AF601746

Every
Baby is
Different
Every
Baby is
Great!

Every Baby is Different, Every Baby is Great!

This book is a work of fiction and non-fiction. Characters, locations, businesses organizations, places, events and incidents are either the product of the author's imagination or are used fictitiously. Any resemblance to an actual person, living or dead, events or locales is entirely coincidental.

For more information contact: Benjamin Mata

ISBN: 978-0-578-98315-8 (Paperback)

Illustration by Brittany Hethcoat © 2021

Dedication

To my little twin:

Thank you for inspiring me to be better. Nothing of value comes easy, and I know you'll understand this in time. May you take the lessons life throws at you and navigate them with appreciation. It's amazing what words can do.

Use them wisely.

-Love Dad

Babies come in all different colors an sizes.

When they're born,

parents feel like they won the best prizes.

Some are born small,

some are born big,

some like big watermelons,

and some like small figs.

Some are born dark, some are born peach,

and others are light.

One thing's for sure, when babies cry,

they cry with great might.

Some have eyes that are small like little almonds,

some have eyes that are big like red grapes,

others have differences, but none have mistakes.

There are some with big beautiful lashes.

There are some with almost none.

What is most important

is the loving is never done.

When Ben Mata discovered his affinity for the power of words He decided he would share it in a way that reaches us all.

Ben is the author of *Every Baby is Different, Every Baby is Great !* He enjoys spending time with his family, photography, and traveling

Brittany Hethcoat is a senior graphic design student at Cal State University, Fullerton

She is the illustrator of *Every Baby is Different, Every Baby is Great !* Brittany loves to draw, play tennis, and have fun with her little brothers.